CW00504346

SIVAN KARNIELI w
She loved eurythmy
philosophy and psycl
trained as a eurythn. _ .... pro-
fessional work includes education, adult education and stage performance. With her latest book
Unternehmung Eurythmie ('Eurythmy Enterprise') she offers
eurythmy in the workplace and also as a remedy for daily stress.
She is married and lives near Basel. Her website is:
www.unternehmung-eurythmie.com

NINA-SOPHIA JUTARD-GRAEWE was born in
Goettingen, Germany, in 1980. She studied paint-
ing at the Assenza painting school in Muenchestein
from 2002 to 2006. Her daughter was born in 2007.
She has been working as an art teacher at the Rudolf
Steiner school in Basel since 2009.

EVERYDAY EURYTHMY

Exercises to Calm, Strengthen and Centre

A Workbook for Daily Practice

Sivan Karnieli

With drawings by Nina-Sophie Jutard-Graewe

RUDOLF STEINER PRESS

Rudolf Steiner Press
Hillside House, The Square
Forest Row, RH18 5ES

www.rudolfsteinerpress.com

First published in English translation by Rudolf Steiner Press, 2016

Originally published under the title *Wer sich bewegt, kommt zu sich selbst,
Eurythmie für jeden Tag* by Futurum Verlag, Basel, 2013

Translated from German by Matthew Barton

*The Publishers are grateful to the Anthroposophical Society in Great Britain as
well as various eurythmy trainings in England for their sponsorship of the
translation*

© Futurum Verlag 2013
This translation © Rudolf Steiner Press 2016

Illustration credits: figs. 4, 5, 6, 7, 18, 20, 21, 24 & 25 by Sivan Karnieli;
fig. 17 from Heinrich Cornelius Agrippa's *De Occulta Philosophia libri III*;
all other illustrations by Nina-Sophie Jutard-Graewe

A CIP catalogue record for this book is available from the British Library

ISBN 978 1 85584 487 2

Cover by Morgan Creative featuring a photograph by Charlotte Fischer
Typeset by DP Photosetting, Neath
Printed and bound by 4Edge Ltd., Essex

Contents

Introduction with Some Practical Tips

I'll say it straight away: eurythmy, if you have heard of it at all, is more than you may realize. It is certainly different from how it usually appears. It is a certain way of thinking, perceiving, experiencing and acting, and relates to many life questions. But rather than diving in to a long explanation, let's get going first and try two exercises. One of them I call the 'Momo exercise', the other the 'apple tree'.

The Momo exercise

The question at the heart of this exercise is, 'What is the source of time?' In the well-known book *Momo* by Michael Ende, there are time-bank agents who itemize how much time people waste every hour, day, week, year, and in the whole of their lives on things that have no point or purpose. These calculations make people feel pressurized into adopting the agents' value system and agreeing to become a client at the time savings bank. Their mere agreement is enough: they don't have to sign a contract since they're already meeting its conditions.

So what is the source of time? Momo, a child who can ask such questions and listen out for answers, eventually finds his way to the Time Being. He learns this secret: that its source is in the human heart. Time becomes life — a living time rather than a fixed quota. Time is not given us from without, but unfolds within us...

To find the source of time, we can do the following.

Find a comfortable sitting position, close your eyes and try to become tranquil. Don't especially focus on your breathing, just breathe calmly. Feel your heart. Feel it to be much larger than its apparent physical form. Rather than on your left side, feel it to be at your centre. It has something of the quality of a flower. Perceive its petals and sense how delicate they are, although not in the least frail; how they resonate with your breath; how your soul fills the flower on the inbreath and is released on the outbreath. Now put all your being into this motion and feel how light arises, pulsing and streaming from the source of your heart, a light full of warmth and forming strength. As it streams into your arms, these move with the motions and forms of your will. Your upper body is also carried by this motion. In this will is life. And this life is time. It pours from your heart.

Time is not outside us — or only in relation to space where, for instance, it is depicted on a clock's face and hands, or when I define a distance by the time I take to cover it. Likewise the terms used in the description of this 'Momo exercise' do not point to anything external. I have looked for thoughts that express the feeling that sets me in motion when I immerse myself in this process. These are pictures, sense images, but ones founded in real experience.

That is the first exercise. It is already a first approach to eurythmy, as is the next.

The apple tree exercise

There is a small apple tree in our garden. It is old now but still only a little taller than me. It bears the best apples I know: coupling sweet and sour, they are crisp and juicy. But they take a long time to ripen, and you can only pick them in late autumn. When I think of this tree what am I really thinking of? For me, our apple tree is a being with whom I can speak. But to do so I must first think differently.

This exercise involves thinking 'apple tree' as a movement rather than as label or static designator. The latter is how we

2

continually think and perceive; or rather we scarcely perceive anything any more. If we think of the apple tree more in terms of movement, we also perceive it more fully. Thinking becomes an organ of perception for the being of the apple tree. This is a thinking in which we also *feel*; and we can only think in this way at all because our *will* is active in it. This kind of thinking, therefore, encompasses both feeling and inner impetus.

Inwardly picture the apple tree, therefore, in late winter with bare branches and gnarled bark. (Of course you could also go out and look at an actual tree. And you can do the same exercise with a different plant—say a flower bulb or even a seed.) Now create in yourself the picture of its ripe fruit hanging on the branches. Then—something that may offend your mundane thinking—feel the apple to be the source of the tree.

Try to have a vivid picture of the ripe apples already hanging invisibly on the winter apple boughs, the blue sky arching overhead, and the warm sun. Picture the forces being drawn up: spring comes (though autumn is already present in the background); the buds open, the subtlest pink blossom appears. Soon the first, bright green leaves emerge, and grow ever larger and darker. The petals fall off, and tiny fruits appear, hard and green. The tree grows out into its surroundings, into warmth and light. Now you can no longer picture the tree at all without its surroundings, without the strength of the soil, the water coursing through it, the light which 'bewitches' it, the warmth that enfolds it...

What is a tree? The answer no longer seems so straightforward. Our 'objective gaze' had only a single perspective. Our 'movement gaze' sees development and relationship. A tree is not a tree without the earth, water, air and sun.

You can do this exercise with anything—with your own life or that of another human being, or a situation. You can also do it with a concept such as 'work'. The exercise can become an outlook on life, a mode of seeing, a particular—or should we say non-particular?—way of thinking.

It seems to me that this way of thinking would help us to solve problems we seem unable to deal with because of the lack of movement in our thought habits.

Now we have come a step closer to eurythmy. It has something intrinsically to do with ourselves. It is something we can practise, and Rudolf Steiner, who brought eurythmy to life a hundred years ago, wanted it to help us learn to think with greater mobility, to look at the world from within rather than only externally. But to do so also means that you become part of what you experience and perceive.

This book arose from the wish to offer a form of eurythmy that everyone can practise for themselves, at home, every day— something we can do that helps us step back from daily concerns and then engage with them again all the more vigorously.

You don't need any prior knowledge. What you need is: yourself, your own perceptions, the courage to try out the movements, the quest for connection and harmony.

It is good to get a pair of gym shoes or non-slip socks. You should wear comfortable clothes. And you should have enough room to move, preferably so you can take a few steps in any direction. However, it is also true to say that the less outer space available the greater will your inner movement be, and this makes you versatile!

You'll need a little time, too, so you can get into a calm space, concentrate for a while and involve yourself fully in the movements.

Here are a few guidelines:

- If you already know the exercises, depending on their nature and your focus, 5 minutes will be enough to carry out one to two exercises.
- You can learn a new exercise, or deepen your acquaintance

4

with one in 10 minutes, but in the same time you could also do a sequence of exercises one after the other. The exercise units listed on pages 83ff will take between 5 to 15 minutes, depending on your skill.

- It is also perfectly fine to practise for half an hour or a whole hour! This will give you time to concentrate more deeply on an exercise, to experience its various aspects at first hand, and deepen a process.

The effect of the exercises can become very apparent in only a little time if you succeed in really penetrating their reality. Or you might occasionally find that you spend a lot of time on them but don't get really get into the swing of it, and that therefore there's little benefit. If this should happen, don't worry, it's normal. Things don't always go equally well each time. At least you have practised, and even that has an effect in itself. Practice does not necessarily mean doing something well, but often just having an *intention* to pursue something.

Reality

I keep pondering on what the word 'reality' means for me. So here I would like briefly to consider the reality we can become aware of through eurythmy, which can repeatedly motivate and inspire us to look at things again and differently, including for instance the many exercises described in this book. This reality has at least four levels! Behind the reality of space is that of time, behind time the reality of feeling, and behind that the reality of intention.

- At the physical, spatial level we are aware of facts, shapes, forms. In this reality we look upon things from without. We look from a particular perspective, a certain standpoint. Here everything has already become what it is.

5

- At the level of time we experience processes by virtue of our thinking. What is developing or has finished developing can be understood and accompanied in our thinking. Thinking itself is movement, process.
- At the level of feeling we experience the feeling that accompanies a process or even instigates it. At the level of facts this kind of reality appears as quality or emanation. (We all know this: two things outwardly the same, and yet they engender a quite different mood in us.)
- In the reality of intention we form resolves, make decisions, choose the direction to go in, create spaces through consciousness. At this level we become responsible for the physical facts that we ourselves have created or are creating. Here we meet ideas in the world. We feel addressed inwardly. When we perceive an idea or a being we are no longer looking at it from without but are seeing the world from within.

In daily life these realities are all completely intertwined and often we are unaware of them. (We can ask how often we have quarrelled with someone or completely missed each other's point because we were confusing the levels...)

But they are also sometimes distinct and separate: for instance when I know that I ought not to do something and yet still do it, or when I am full of ideals and fail to make any of them real.

These levels of reality are interacting dimensions.[1] We're familiar with the three dimensions broadening from the point to the straight line, from the straight line to the plane and from the plane to three-dimensional space. Through our capacity to stand upright and move we develop into these spatial conditions. We are centred in a sense of space.

But what are the fourth, fifth and sixth dimensions? In mathematical terms, positive space becomes negative; or in other words, what was filled with matter now becomes filled with spirit.

The first spirit-filled dimension, and the fourth in mathematics, is what we experience as time. From this dimension onwards, cause works out of the future towards us. Since the fifth dimension is apparent as feeling, this means that time must become the *experience* of time if we wish to be aware of it. Only in inner experience is time a distinct reality (otherwise we can only ever perceive it through space and spatial processes).[2] Thus the dimension of feeling opens up within time.

Feeling, in turn, acquires its focus through consciousness. Presence of mind arises in feeling that encompasses and at the same time organizes the whole: the sixth dimension is not the focused point but the point's periphery. This means that by creating this dimension in eurythmy through our own activity we can comprehend the idea as something working actively out of the future, and engage with it through our whole being, with our thinking, feeling and will. We no longer comprehend it as idea (ideas belong to the third dimension) but as energy. Idea has been active since time immemorial — how else could we progress towards it?

Through eurythmy we gradually gain access to these realities, learn to know and recognize them, to distinguish, connect and move within them — as soul, spirit and body. All dimensions of the *single* reality are at work simultaneously, but the last dimension (that of intention) is, basically, the first in spiritual terms: we make a decision (to take a particular route for instance). In most cases this decision immediately becomes action and occupies space, becomes a fact and reality. But we only gain inner freedom through an experience of the movement active between idea and spatial reality — when we notice that we are pursuing a path from intention to the goal itself, and shaping this path too. My feeling is neither the instigator nor the side effect of this movement but an organ of perception.

I will keep referring to these levels in my description of the exercises; but I did not assign each exercise to one of these four levels since feeling always acts as a guiding star, leading movements towards the idea.

1. The Technique of Eurythmy is Love

The word 'upright' also contains the sense of 'moral uprightness' or honesty. A person who stands upright is potentially authentic in his own and others' eyes. This 'upright' position is the starting position for all eurythmy exercises. Eurythmy counteracts mendacity, said Rudolf Steiner. Someone who is upright cannot easily lie.

This small observation can already show us something else: in eurythmy the soul's inner movement and the body's outer movement are one. The technique of eurythmy is not about muscle tension or a particular mobility of the body, but love. From this technique proceeds what can then be perceived as movement impetus, tension,

Starting position for the exercises
Unless otherwise indicated, every exercise starts by placing yourself in space in an upright but not stretching position; your arms should hang loosely by your side. Try to feel calm, at rest. Your feet are close enough to each other to nearly touch, and your weight rests equally on both.

release, presence, immediacy and a great deal more. The soul's love should be active in this technique. In common parlance people say that love is blind, but the opposite is true: when we love, we see more because love opens the eyes of the soul. Love is a movement towards the things and the beings of the world...

And isn't it this that increasingly enriches us? If I do my gymnastics exercises in the morning, my body becomes or remains more mobile, flexible and stronger, and I will of course feel good. But if I start my day with 'soul gymnastics' (as Steiner also called eurythmy), my *soul* becomes more mobile, flexible and stronger. Everything I encounter will move me more deeply. I will sense the richness of life, my own included. Above all, I will give my soul its own space to exist: the stronger my own inner capacity for movement, the less the outer world will overwhelm me. Perhaps things will still be hectic, but this will impinge less and less on me. *I* will not feel hectic. I am on my path, walking it myself, rather than being pulled from one place to the next. I begin to see the beauty of the world and to feel its abundance. I do not think one thing yet do another. I can be creatively present in my life, living, thinking, feeling and acting in the here and now.

The most important question — one which sustains eurythmy — is this: who is it in me who can stand upright, who is capable of loving, who opens up spaces and shapes them?

> Let us speak of the I, the authentic I. Let us try. What I call the I is the movement, the impulse that enables me to employ the four elements of this earth on which I live, but also my intelligence and the motions of my sensibility, even my dreams. It is, in fact, a strength that lends me the power nothing else gives me: that is, the power of not having to wait for outward life to approach me before I live. The ego needs things, the greatest possible number of them (whether these be money, status, authority, acclaim or gratification). The I does not seek these. When it is present, at work, active, then it sets its own work against this other world of things. The I is wealth in the midst of poverty; it is interest when everything around us is tedium. It is hope even if all objective means of hope have faded. From it arises humankind's whole world of inventiveness. And ultimately it is what we retain when all else is denied, when nothing more approaches us from without, and yet our powers are still great enough to overcome this emptiness.[3]

These words are by Jacques Lusseyran, who was blinded age four. He also said: '... real blindness was the inability to love any more, or to grieve; it was not the loss of sight.'[4]

To raise oneself into the upright, to love, to see, even if not with one's eyes, to feel and engender the future within us now: all the substance of a world that is growing all the time. A world of growing, that is what eurythmy is, and this becomes life: a world that is founded on the human I, on the strength that can face the void even, since someone—my I—is still there and perceives it.

The following little exercise helps to come to oneself in the middle of the daily rush. You don't have to do the whole of it; sometimes it is enough to feel my head consciously in the pillar of light, and perceive my backspace. I can do this while waiting at a train station, while walking in town in a large throng of people, or when my little boy has a tantrum. Our frontspace absorbs our attention (and in seeing we often immediately form ideas) while the backspace releases us. Here we can listen in to openness. Our frontspace is defined, earthly, material; our backspace is not yet determined (we ourselves determine it as we enter into the world before us). It is spiritual, invisible. The frontspace takes myself from me while the backspace gives me myself.

Exercise: finding the upright

Stand relaxed, your feet together or very slightly apart, and let your head and shoulders/arms follow gravity so that they hang down in front. Your knees too should be loose, relaxed.

Now kindle a power of light in you, which passes from the heart and broadens. (That is the real meaning of 'uprightness'.) Follow this trail of light which simultaneously travels upwards and downwards. The stronger we engender it in us, the more powerfully will its momentum encompass our body, so that we gradually stretch and straighten. Stretching does not mean pulling away from below but rather strengthening and warming the feeling of your lower body and releasing yourself in an upwards direction—until last of all you raise your head into the column of light. Now feeling and body have become one. Space becomes free immediately around you; the backward space especially comes to awareness. Gravity is overcome: you stand upright, sustained by space.

If you now direct your focus, your consciousness—or, I could also say, the light—to the area between your shoulder blades, you can experience your arms becoming lighter so that you can raise them sideways into the horizontal almost with a sense of weightlessness, as if they are carried by the periphery.

This experience can suggest the ancient symbol of the sun—a circle with a dot in the middle ⊙ —which becomes here an inner picture of the free human being.[5]

Make sure that:

- stretching and straightening does not become tension, but that, as it were, light still flows through the muscles. If you are too tense, the flow is inhibited. Then it is like putting stones in the bed of a stream that obstruct the current;
- equilibrium does not become static or rigid, but remains a continual and simultaneous creating, finding and perceiving of the light.

2. The Outer World is Within Me

Everything in the world is a part of us; there is nothing that cannot be expressed through us.[6]

Rudolf Steiner

The next exercise involves an inward movement from creature-hood to the Creator. It is a soul gymanistics, a meditation, a developing awareness of our humanity. We are born out of the divine world, and a new world will emerge from us — one in which freedom exists.

We can see from our capacity to stand upright that we have the potential for freedom in us, and that it is our destiny. This is a picture, which nature's language offers us, of the concept 'freedom'. At the same time it is a metaphor for the fact that we are endowed with an I. Whenever we say 'I' and accompany this with body language, we inevitably stretch or straighten a little. No one would think of accompanying this word with bowing or bending! Thus, when we speak it, we emphasize our capacity and power to be upright.

Likewise we can learn to perceive this power in language itself. In the sound 'ee' (German 'i' in the word 'ich') we straighten and grow brighter; we feel within us the power that raises us upright and experiences the I. The sound 'ee' is indeed present in the word for 'I' in many languages (e.g. 'yo' and 'io' in Spanish and Italian, the English word moves from the 'ah' to the 'ee').

Every vowel and consonant has a connection with the for-mative forces in us and the world. Nature and human being both offer pictures of dynamic qualities which becomes audible in language. By hearkening to these qualities we can grasp pro-

13

cesses that act or take effect in reality. Language is infinitely more than mere information! It is energy, activity. This is why eurythmy is also called 'visible speech', and also why the following exercise is called 'I A O'.

In this exercise one starts to hearken to the power of these sounds: 'ee' ('I'), 'ah' ('A') and 'oh' ('O'). This chord, as we can call it, reveals the free human being between past and future, between origin and goal, alpha and omega and between the world as it has so far developed, and as it can still become.

I A O exercise[*]

The human form, the feet and feeling.

I ('ee')

From the starting position of a loose, relaxed, upright stance first find the place where the balls of both feet rest on the ground. Find a point of free equilibrium above this point, and inwardly connect it, without lowering your head, with the point at the root of the nose. In this stance experience yourself as pillar. It is important to really *feel* this balance, both outwardly and inwardly. Rest fully in yourself and at the same time in the whole world.

Now try to engender within you a mood of quiet joy: 'I am fully present in myself, and my heart is alive and joyous'. This too is a stretching and straightening into light, but inwardly now. Feel this strength fully. Stretch both upwards and downwards in it, always creating and maintaining balance. Make sure you stay

---

[*] This is the first speech-sound exercise that Rudolf Steiner gave in eurythmy: here we only move our human form in standing without as yet moving a form in space. Rudolf Steiner, lecture on 24 June 1924, in: *Eurythmie als sichbare Sprache* (GA 279), Rudolf Steiner Verlag, Dornach 2005, p. 161. (*Eurythmy as Visible Speech*, Rudolf Steiner Press 1984.)

fully with yourself and do not lose yourself in motion. The feeling is one in which the vigour of your heart becomes so great that your whole form becomes filled with light. But to grow brighter in this way you must at the same time become deeper, must make the strength of your form a vessel for this light.

A ('ah')

A different feeling arises when you listen in to the space behind you. In doing so, shift your weight from the balls of the feet to the heels without losing the upright pillar. *Your whole form* will shift slightly backwards.

Repeat this movement—of simply shifting your weight—a few times, increasingly attending to the inner experience rather than the physical process. Then you will discover that the power in a sense freely available in the 'ee' sound now becomes bound to the body. It draws inwards, grows denser below. In the 'ee' the heavens were in a sense *within* you; but now the heavens open *above* you.

From above, from far away, light streams into me. I receive it through my open stance in space; it is as if my form is created and shaped by this light.

This feeling is the inward aspect of the 'A': the self-receiving human being.

O ('oh')

Lastly, shift your weight to the toes (without actually standing on tip-toe). If we hung a plumb line from the point on your forehead it would now fall *in front* of the balls of the feet. But you are still upright, without any bend or 'kink' in your form. How do you perceive the world now? How do you relate to your surroundings?

You can as it were shift position merely physically, or also

15

effect it inwardly by engendering within you the sense that someone calls you, that something draws you outwards—but that *you* still wish to follow this call, and thus give yourself an inner impulse to do so.

Attend to what happens inwardly when you shift your weight; then you feel how a stream of forces extends beyond you. Yet still keep yourself within it: do not keel forwards, nor place yourself on your toes, but shape this stream with the strength of your being.

The heart is full of warmth: the feeling of presence streams outwards and fills the space that is created by this feeling. That is the quality of 'O'.

Finally, release the exertion so that you now stand there relaxed, allowing the exercise to go on resonating.

I A O with arm movements

The exercise is based on the one above. Here too make sure you are upright, that your weight shifts to different points on the foot (middle—back—front). Likewise attend to relationships between your physical form and life forces (balanced—bound—free) and to the initiating or also answering feeling. The better you know the exercise, and the more you have practised it, the more strongly you can engender this sense, and the more the outer movement can become the expression of an inner dynamic.

This is particularly important when you add the arm movements. They give expression to an inner process, similar to when we accompany speech with gestures. In eurythmy, gesture is artistically enhanced.

I ('ee')

In the 'I', the power of loving presence and illumined equilibrium becomes so great that your arms are drawn both upwards and downwards into its stream, until you stand there with one arm upwards, the other downwards (it doesn't matter which does which). Both are experienced in connection with each other. The hands also give expression to this feeling: the upper one radiates light through the palm, and is extended, while the other forms a small vessel and creates (counter)weight. The legs can also open a little in a small forward step, so that balance is better supported below.

Make sure that the gesture always corresponds to your centre, and that the stream that forms it is always nourished from there. Your being is not bounded or limited by the gesture; it is an expression of your being when this connects from within with the world's light.

Fig. 1 I ('ee')

A ('ah')

As you form the 'A', feel how light streams in from above, from far away, and move towards it with strong, open, extended hands and opening arms. Form an angle with your arms and experience this angle as you lead your arms upwards as extension of your form. Make sure that you do not lose the position of weight on your heels. Your upper body will tend to bend slightly backwards to avoid this happening. The more you extend the arms the more strongly you can feel connected with something

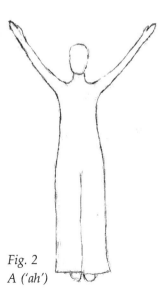

Fig. 2
A ('ah')

17

higher which, as you move towards it, at the same time descends towards you.

You can then lower your opened arms (keeping them extended) or, as variation, direct them downwards from the outset in a not too narrow and not too broad angle, so that you have the feeling that light flows from above and through your figure, streaming into the earth.

O ('oh')

Fig. 3 O ('oh')

Finally with the 'O' you direct the stream and the strength of your being into the world. Starting from the heart your arms follow a warm stream in front of you out into the frontspace as if embracing it, forming a closed, round O form. In this forming gesture you preserve your own self and individuality in your devotion to the world.

The rounded 'O' gesture can be formed above the head, horizontally in front of you or downwards. An inner picture as you do this can embody the direction. (Words such as dome, gold, morning, moat, cloak, tomb can help us to develop an inner sense of this gesture.)

Additional aspects

• Note how a counterspace to the physical movement is created. If you shift your weight backwards, the frontspace becomes larger—*it is still open for your deeds.* If you shift the weight forwards, the space behind you grows larger — *it gives strength for your actions.*

- Feel in the 'O' the strength which enables you to become everything yourself, and through which you can say to everything in the world: 'I am this. I am the gold and the morning.' What you utter, you become.

In summary we can say that in the 'I' I feel the immediacy of the present moment: I am free. The 'A' is what has previously existed, and now lives in me as experience, forming a foundation for future perspectives. This is never a matter of cast-iron fate or guilt but of developmental potential. I encompass this through the source of the heart in 'O'. Here I create my reality myself. I create a reality that I can *will* and intend. I bring the future into the world through myself.

'The world is not outside me — I am it myself.' This phrase can only be uttered by someone who does not experience the world as something separate from him but recognizes that he himself is the world, and that he can help shape it through his individuality. Helping to shape the world is the same as working together. A co-worker is more than an employee. A person who collaborates is spiritually free: what he does is what he wills and intends. In our own biography this means that we give ourselves from within; everything which comes towards us (seemingly from without) is deeply connected with us, belongs intrinsically to us. Outer and inner form a unity in our I. Strokes of destiny become opportunities in life, faults or flaws become developmental capacity, knowledge becomes the condition for growth, our individuality becomes a resource to draw on.

3. Every Person Wears a Crown

This phrase, which figures in the German campaign publicity for a basic income, offers an apt picture of the inner stance we can experience when we do eurythmy. Every person does indeed wear a crown and rules over the land that he or she embodies. Eurythmy sets me at peace with myself because my soul is governing my body, and my spirit is governing my soul – rather than the other way round! Learning to direct myself from within and experience myself as the centre of my life, my attention is present in what I do – in my thinking, feeling and actions. I am the queen or king of my domain.

The following exercise seeks equilibrium in movement, in walking. It has a harmonizing, balancing and calming effect. As we walk, our centre becomes free and the heart opens. Nothing draws us out of ourselves: neither what lies before nor what lies behind us. The centre is the place where each person can determine his life, where we find the source of action, and where space can appear – space that enables me to speak or sing from within (instead of being a note 'struck' from without, like a gong).

Exercise: Threefold walking

Take a little step forwards and in this position place yourself upright and firmly on the ground with the weight distributed equally between both feet. Your gaze looks forward.

Now feel yourself to be on a path that leads you forward, and make an inner decision to take this path.

The back foot and the heel release themselves from the ground and the weight shifts to your front foot.

- Experience what happens in the soul as you release the foot from the ground! Outwardly almost nothing happens but inwardly a whole new world dawns. The frontspace in a sense enters you so that you become one with what is already present in the future.
- You can also experience how you enter into complete harmony with yourself: Now I am free, and can place the back foot wherever I wish. At this moment the path is open before me and can be determined: I am walking it and creating it simultaneously by walking. In this phase of the step I am most upright.

Now, still experiencing the unfolding path, carry forward the foot you have released entirely from the ground and feel the lifted heel being carried by a stream released through your decision. This stream comes out of the earth, curves over the ground and sinks back into the earth again as you place your foot once more on the earth (rising again at the same time as you lift the other foot).

Place the carried foot on the ground and thus connect anew with the earth. You touch the ground first of all with your toes, and following them the foot also descends. Try to perceive the ground as you touch down into it, and feel the weight at this point equally distributed between both feet.

Again a quite different mood can be experienced in the soul. You now connect trustingly with the earth, and the decision manifests in the world through deed. The state of complete accord with myself is once again released: I have passed through, and the stream from the future ebbs away behind me.

For every step you can silently speak a line from a verse by Rudolf Steiner.[7]

> I feel my destiny — my destiny finds me
> I feel my star — my star finds me
> I feel my aims — my aims find me

Flow in the step

Flowing threefold walking is based on this conscious stepping, but now the steps continually flow into one another. As you place one foot down, the other is already being lifted, so that the stream from the past, which sustains me, meets the stream from the future. My own resolve (whose source lies in the future!) leads me onwards. Walking becomes flow, a river upon which I 'swim'.

Naturally this stepping is not limited to walking forwards. It can be done in any direction.

Practice options

- Changing or doubling the tempo. For instance, one takes 4 slow steps, then 8 quicker ones in the same time, and again 16 in the same time (the quicker you move, the smaller each step will become).
- Immediately after this, return to just 4 steps. This gives an inner sense of time and unity, and is likewise a musical experience.

Variation with arm movements

If you can experience this stream through the feet, you are likely to want to move your arms also. The simplest variation is another threefold movement, in which you can freely choose how to combine the arm and feet movements.

For instance, you can:

- take *one step* with its three phases along with *one phase of the arm movement*;
- coordinate the three phases *of one step* with the *three phases of the arm movement*;

- take *three* or even more *steps* in the same time as *one phase of the arm movement.*
- etc.

The threefold arm movement is based on the three planes of space (see Fig. 4). Try to feel these three planes of space passing through you so that their common intersection point is where every person points to when he refers to himself as 'I'.

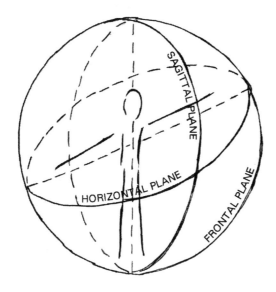

Fig. 4 The human being in the three planes of space

Let your arms hang loose and begin in the sagittal plane by raising your arms forwards until you reach the horizontal level, thus forming a quarter circle.

When you reach the horizontal plane, change direction and open your arms by spreading them outwards in this plane.

When you reach the plane that divides front from back, known as the frontal plane, bring your arms sideways together again above your head.

Thus there are three phases in each plane.

Now you can begin again anew from above downward, in the opposite direction (quarter circle of the arms to reach the horizontal plane, then spreading outwards and finally bringing both arms back down again into the starting position).

Be aware:

- of the whole circle, even if you are only making a quarter of it visible at any moment;
- of the changes of direction, which should be precise and not vague — grasp them actively (this gives inner, self-governing coherence);
- of the process rather than the end-goal of the movement, which also means assigning equal time to each of the phases so that they unfold evenly — this is something you have to *do* rather than think, and it will give you a sense of mastery;
- of the distance between the starting point and the end point of a movement direction — the distance from the starting point grows larger, that towards the end-point smaller (this gives inner breadth and overview).

Practice options:

- Hold your hands differently each time; this will enable you to perceive to what extent they are an organ of perception for space, and how your relationship to space alters in consequence:

  turn your hands *downwards or upwards* in the sagittal plane,
  turn them *towards each other, away from each other, or upwards* in the horizontal plane,
  turn them *upwards, downwards or forwards* in the frontal plane.

- In standing perform the arm movement in 'canon', i.e. begin for instance by raising the right arm from below in the sagittal plane, then do the same with the left arm when the right begins the second path in the horizontal plane.
- Do this arm 'canon' in walking.

4. Do We Still Feel Our Lives?

If we consider the rising divorce rates, the isolation of millions of people in front of their screens each evening, the search for ever more extreme experiences in the world of sport, or the anonymity of city life where thudding noise levels cover an underlying emptiness, it becomes clear that many people today are living in a way that numbs rather than sensitizes them.

Again we are led to the point of asking: Can we create connections? Can we form relationships? Can we use our time creatively, or even actually make time? The only person who can do this is me myself, with my interests, creativity, thinking, feeling and will.

Today we are repeatedly faced with the question of the I. Whether we really experience our lives, or allow ourselves to do so, is a question of the I too. This is why the first of the following exercises is also called 'I am the path'.

This means roughly: 'I myself am my path, I am my own destiny, for I myself bring my reality, my experience into the world'. Whatever we do, whether thinking, feeling or acting, becomes reality; and this, as Joseph Beuys famously said, is because every person is an artist, a being destined to be creative, one who creates reality.

In contrast to the 'threefold walking' exercise, the focus in the first exercise is more on the form. How does a form become process? How can one transform form as rigid outer shape into a dynamic?

In the other exercises the aim is to engender active feelings. Feelings express themselves in a gesture that is pictorial. Try to become a picture *in* the gesture, experience this picture, create it yourself, strengthen it through inner activity, and finally, absorb the strength into which you have entered—for your inner movement is a gateway.

Exercise: I am the path

Place yourself first consciously into the three dimensions of external space. Raise yourself upright and feel this upright position between below and above. Then perceive a world in front of you and a world behind, and then finally the fact that you stand centrally between left and right.

I experience space because my form places me into this space, because the same principle that is active in me is also at work in what I perceive around me.[8]

Spatial awareness

The exercise begins with the spatial awareness you created above; with this awareness you then move the following form: three steps forward, three steps back.[*] The anchor-point of space is in you yourself.

A feeling arises which enables you to experience, 'I am space'. Wherever I go I create it, it arises through me. We could also say: 'I govern myself, I am not pulled by outer necessity from one point to another.'

The most important capacity here is that of being upright. This is like a plumb line, a continual orientation, and only through it do we gain a spatial relationship in and with the world. It is a guideline in the midst of space. To preserve this uprightness, it can be helpful to direct feeling and awareness to your back, and perceive this and surrounding space.

---

[*] This form, in which a path forward and back is experienced as a unity, is an 'I' form if I do it alone, and a 'we' form if I do it with several others in a circle, thus also experiencing community with them.

27

Path awareness and the dual stream

To develop path awareness, no longer just walk from point A to point B but instead let A and B become the focuses of your awareness, places where the process changes because *you* change it. Only in spatial awareness are A and B physical, material points. In path or process consciousness they are subject to your creative power.

In this way you can now 'release' yourself into space: you form and encompass A and B with your awareness and maintain yourself in this whole context wherever you may be on the path. It is a bit like the egg yolk held in the egg-white. The centre is now defined by the periphery. This inversion (placing yourself consciously into space —

becoming 'centred' out of space) is something you can accomplish a few times in standing until you gain a sense of what this means. It will give rise to an (initially) inward movement. When you feel this strongly enough, give way to it and become the path.

- Can you perceive the difference between the first and second part of the exercise, between spatial awareness and path awareness? The first part is always associated with distinct and separate 'moments': each step must be taken anew, each change of direction must continually be determined in the here and now.

- If you can find your way through to an experience of the second part of the exercise, that of path awareness, life forces flow towards you. You are then held within a larger context. This however is not something mystical but an expanded awareness by means of which you sustain yourself from the periphery. The activity you employ here is what you experience as movement, and into which you then also enter physically.

Fig. 5 Path awareness with counterstream

Now direct your attention to the path as such. It can be helpful if you say to yourself, 'I am the path.'

What are you doing inwardly here? Your awareness has to go out ahead of you so that you are always further on than you are physically, engendering continual activity within yourself... If you do not do this, in a sense you are excluding yourself, and you fall (back) immediately into separate, isolated steps. In path reality you are always part of a whole. You immerse yourself in the process and experience yourself *within* time.

Goal and starting point are contained in the path and manifest through it.

Applied to walking backwards and forwards, in 'technical' terms this means that as you walk between point A and point B you focus on how the distance to B grows smaller while that from A grows larger. As you walk forwards, the path backwards already, as it were, approaches you; and when you walk backwards, try to feel how the forward path in a sense passes through you. Perceive

29

The dual stream of time
The dual stream of time is a phenomenon which we actually know in ordinary life, but which we may often be unaware of. The stream of time flowing from the past is apparent in the particular configuration of where we come from and what we are meant to become. In ideals that become our yearning and inner striving, we meet the opposite stream of time, coming from the future. This is not to be found anywhere in the outer world but only within us. We bear the future within us by virtue of our capacity to create or recreate ourselves. The past is immutable, the future is our destiny that continually acts in the present. The walking person is an image of this present moment within the dual stream of time.

both these at once and you deepen your experience of process: you stand and move within it.[9] In this way you can begin to experience the dual stream of time.

The exercise can be simplified in the following way:

- Three steps forward, three steps back;
- focus your awareness on the point in front;
- focus your awareness on the point behind;
- focus your awareness on both points simultaneously.

When do you feel yourself larger and when smaller? Does the closeness to the point to which your awareness is directed affect this feeling?

Other aspects you can notice, which are all *realities of our own outlook*:

- How does spatial quality alter? Or if there are several people, how does it alter between the members of the group?
- How do you feel when you are in spatial awareness, and how when you are in time awareness?
- How is the quality of breathing (also its resonance in the space around you)?
- Do you become tranquil, calm?

30

- Do things become still in the room? Can you discern the quality and 'sound' of this attention?
- How do you perceive time? How does it change?
- How do you experience yourself, and what effect does this have on your surroundings?
- How is your encounter with the world around you? Is it more confrontational, harmonious or carried by a higher consciousness?

Forms with counterstream

Instead of merely walking a straight line between two points you can enhance the exercise by walking diverse forms. It may make sense to begin with to practise the 'technical aspect', e.g. how do I walk a circle?* Or how do I walk a spiral?

Form elements include: a curve, a circle, a lemniscate (∞-shaped loop), an inward or outward spiral, as well as straight lines in various relationships to each other — triangle, cube, etc.

Once you have mastered the technical aspect of the form, enter into the process. Grasp the form from within as a whole and move out of this wholeness. From this wholeness flow arises. In this flow of movement a dynamic will develop in certain forms, since form is the expression of a particular consciousness that works into it in a living way. The form itself can only reveal its nature and begin to speak when a person enters into it consciously and starts to experience it as an energy form — as in the following exercise.

Example of the counterstream: spiralling inwards and outwards

To illustrate the experience of the counterstream, let us take the spiral form, which we can walk either inwards or outwards.

---

*See the exercise 'Cross form with circle' in Chapter 9.

When we spiral inwards the counterstream comes towards us continually from the centre, and we create an uninterrupted tension between without and within. This means that the centre of the form enters your consciousness from the outset as feeling within your own centre. Your intention forms this centre, otherwise you would be unable even to begin to move the form. The goal of your movement instigates its source and impetus, and determines the path's direction. (The reverse is true too: the source of movement creates the goal, for in spiritual terms the point transforms into the periphery and encompasses the whole.)

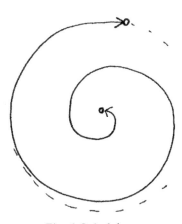

Fig. 6 Spiral forms

As you approach the centre of the spiral, the periphery grows ever larger because the feeling of the centre that you engendered in yourself at the beginning, becomes ever more spatially identified, and so powers of awareness are released for your surroundings.

Correspondingly, as we spiral outwards again, the centre becomes increasingly apparent, and its pull or charge ever stronger.

Exercise: Light streams upwards — weight bears downwards

Once again we start from the upright position. Sense and enliven in you a power of light that streams upwards, and raise your arms sideways into this stream until they form a vessel — not too narrow and not too wide — opening upwards; or something like a 'receptacle' for the light. The extending hands serve as a kind of plough making a path to the desired angle of the arms. The palms are turned inwards as you do this, and a slight muscle tension can be felt in both arms and hands: *light streams upwards.*

Now create the counterweight to this movement, without losing the light, by opening your legs sideways into an angle that equals that of your arms; follow this form with your awareness and let it flow downwards from the hips: *weight bears downwards.*

You can let these two movements follow very quickly in succession, and thus enter into a dual force field. This field is the reality of life substance (ether force) and matter, in which we stand as long as we live, though usually unconsciously.

To place oneself consciously into this reality and to encompass it requires and at the same time redeems the power at our centre that makes us truly human. But this does not occur directly at the soul level but at the etheric or life level. New life forces can enter us through the solar plexus.

Make sure that:

- you keep your weight balanced evenly in the middle between back and front, and do not keel backwards;
- that your focused awareness is not held in the solar plexus region where the tips of the two angles made by arms and legs interpenetrate (to ensure this, focus your awareness on the distance or the lines of force between your hands and between your feet).

You can decide yourself how long to remain in this position. It is only worthwhile for as long as you can keep filling it inwardly. Then release this gesture both inwardly and outwardly.

Exercise: Yes — No

In this exercise[*] the frontspace is perceived in relation to the backspace, and vice versa. When we say 'yes' we move inwardly

---

[*] Yes–No is also a eurythmy therapy exercise. If you wish to use it therapeutically, it is advisable to find a eurythmy therapist.

towards what we affirm; when we say 'no', we distance ourselves. We open a gateway to what we say 'yes' to, and close one when we say 'no'.[10]

You can feel your way into this firstly, and also already take a couple of steps backwards or forwards to get a stronger sense of it.

So now imagine something that you say 'yes' to, and picture this with vivid feeling. Now move forwards towards this inner picture you created.

You can likewise call up a picture of something that you negate or deny, and withdraw from it with backward steps.

Midway between these you occupy the 'centre' — in equilibrium.

In eurythmy, 'yes' and 'no' are spoken with the legs and feet since to say these words is also a deed.

Exercise

In the starting position, stand upright with feet together.

For the 'yes', describe with your left leg a half circle forwards,

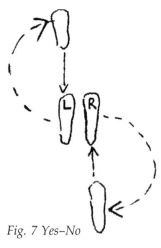

then place the foot on the ground with half your weight on it. Only for a *brief moment* stand there in balance on both feet. Then draw the foot back again in a direct (straight) line to the starting position.

For the 'no', with your right foot again describe a half circle, but this time backwards, once more dividing your weight equally between both feet for a brief moment. Then draw this right foot back again in a straight line to the starting position.

Fig. 7 Yes–No

Perform both movements in alternation, initially practising this slowly but then speeding up the tempo and repeating it eight to twelve times, until finally you stop suddenly and stand there tranquilly.

Make sure that:

- you do not lift your foot higher than necessary when describing the circles close above the ground;
- your upper body stays as calm as possible – try to 'ride' on the legs' movement;
- you do not get tense or rigid, or stuck in your thinking. The legs should remain relaxed, led by your feeling not the head: it is as if you are strongly penetrating warmth, water or will with your 'yes' and 'no', even when the movement gets quicker.

Exercise: A ('ah') – reverence

Nowadays 'reverence' is an attitude of soul that scarcely figures any more. Perhaps we can think back to a childhood experience of looking up to someone or something with wonder and deep feeling. If so, this was a gift for us – a sense that life has deep meaning.

Everything we experience as meaningful makes us healthy.

This may be why the following exercise has a generally health-giving effect. It is an attempt to engender the feeling of reverence *in* and *through* gesture.

Form an 'ah' gesture by raising the arms upwards into forward space in an open angle, and shifting your weight slightly backwards (see page 17). This gesture can give expression to the sense of looking up to something higher that we revere. Hold this for a moment. Then draw back the shoulder blades with an active impetus so that the ribcage expands. This also

35

relaxes tension in the arms, which you move slightly back-wards as if you were throwing a light veil over yourself. Now, as you slowly lower your arms, the veil or the gift given is also lowered...

But you do not need to lower your arms fully: form another 'ah' gesture, release it again; do this several times.

Exercise: Hope – U ('oo')

Hope also has a soul gesture. The following exercise is suitable for helping make it visible.

Stand upright and shift your weight slightly backwards (as for the 'ah'). This opens the frontspace. Your upper arms remain loose by your side. And the hands of the two slightly bent lower arms each form a curved bowl. This is the gesture of hope.

Stand for a moment in this inner movement and outward position. Then decide to find the U ('oo') gesture and shift your weight forwards again until you come into balance. Direct your awareness (but not your eyes) downwards before you. This inner point is retained as focus throughout the whole succeeding movement. Maintain it now, at the same time as shifting your weight, as you raise your arms and hands above and to either side of your head, with arms and hands briefly retaining the rounded 'hope bowls'. Take the whole of the space above you into your gesture, and lead it – with the backs of your hands now touching each other, so that the outside of your arms now point inwards – downwards in front of you to the focal point.

Standing in the upright position, very slightly leaning for-wards after you have completed the downward movement of the arms, pause a moment and then release the pressure in them along with the gesture.

36

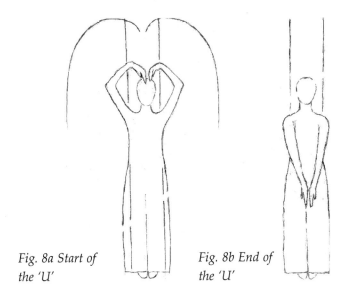

Fig. 8a Start of
the 'U'

Fig. 8b End of
the 'U'

This dual gesture of the 'Hope — U' can be done several times in succession, as can the following exercise, 'Love — E' ('eh'). The 'U' movement embodies the fulfilment of hope, and there is good reason, therefore, why the weight is shifted during it. The frontspace that was open in hope is inwardly encompassed and filled. You can learn to feel in this I impulse of the 'U' movement an enlivening of creative potential; and also that the form of the 'U' conveys a sense of strength within restriction.

Exercise: Love — E ('eh')

As the name of the exercise tells you, it begins with bringing a feeling of love towards the whole world. Stand upright; direct your awareness into the heart and the insides of the hands, which become like eyes and turn towards the world. Feel your fingertips like light feelers opening to the world.

With this in mind, open your arms and spread them out (here we can feel a kind of cloak of warmth from behind enveloping

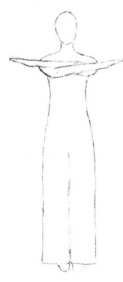

Fig. 9 E ('eh')

the arms). That is the gesture of love. By virtue of your upright form you can feel behind you something great and bright. You too are encompassed in love, and it passes through you. Stand for a moment entirely in the presence of this out-streaming gesture.

Then comes the moment of change, the 'E'. Both arms were spread wide, but now bring them strongly in front of your centre and allow them to cross so that the forearms make clear contact. From breadth to the centre—that is the arms' movement. Your awareness is focused both on the crossing point and on the space that remains open behind you.

Then do the love gesture again; and once again the 'eh'.

Repeat this several times in the same tempo. At the end of the exercise, release the gesture and be still for a moment.

38

5. Moving with Love

The inner hand — a sole no longer walking
except on feeling, holding itself upwards, open
and in its mirror
receiving heavenly roads, the ones
that walk themselves...[11]

Rainer Maria Rilke

When we begin to feelingly grasp the nature of a speech sound, language reveals its miracles. We will begin to understand the spirit of language. How does each language express the same thing differently — for instance what aspect of a tree is expressed in English, German (*Baum*) or French (*arbre*)? If we keep hearkening to our sub-verbal sound experience (and it helps to feel the space our mouth forms, and the movement of the tongue when we speak a word) we discover that *Baum* accentuates or echoes the enveloping crown, that *arbre* conveys the branching, windswept twigs and foliage, while 'tree' has more the quality of something growing tall and upright between heaven and earth, something infused with strength from the whole cosmos.

The spirit of language has an affinity with the landscape it is at home in. The consonants are images of forms, sounds, noises, relationships. As language developed, human beings with their distinctive, differing interiority encompassed and expressed the world they lived in through speech sounds. This gave rise to a configuration of sounds that was still fully imbued with the nature of what they were expressing, albeit mediated by a particular people's inner qualities.

Today we can say that language works back in turn on the

people of a particular region. From this perspective, we can also see it as opening a path to knowledge.

The world, speech and the human being have always belonged most intimately together, and this is still true. Single words, such as AUM or TAO, once had a mystery content. *Speech* itself is a mystery, and the bearer of a spiritual power.

In the following exercises a portal can open for us to access the power of speech sounds. In the way they are described here, in terms of movement, they act on the human being in specific ways. Likewise, our engagement with sound qualities in speech opens us up to diverse aspects of the world and the human being.

Exercises: Speech-sound qualities and healing forces

Liquid L

The L is the only 'liquid sound' in the alphabet. Having the quality of water, it brings a process into flow, and has an enlivening, soul-cleansing quality.

Place one foot slightly forwards and stand upright with relaxed, not straightened knees. Now reach sideways and downwards with your hands (and fingers, which are rounded like bowls) and slowly bring them together as if you are grasping something dense — or also heavy — down in front of you. Try to really perceive the substance of the air below with your hands and lower arms. As your hands come together, the substance between them grows denser. *The body is now leaning slightly forwards.*

Once your hands have come close enough together to grasp the heaviness from below, they form a kind of double bowl. Now

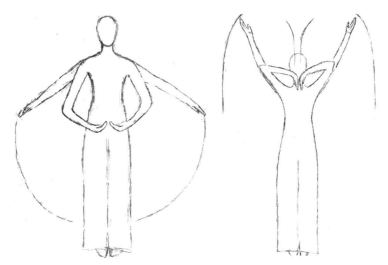

Fig. 10a L – Initial downward
movement

Fig. 10b L – Upward opening
movement

lift this 'substance' vertically upwards to heart height in front of
you, in a kind of scooping movement, the backs of your fingers
pushing against each other and increasingly in closer contact. *As
you do this, shift your weight back to the centre between back and front.*

Now follows a moment of inversion, which in a sense passes
through the heart as if through the eye of a needle. At this
moment of equilibrium you open your back between the
shoulder blades and release gravity upwards into levity: the
movement passes from your shoulder blades into your upper
arms, then engages the lower arms and finally the hands. No
later than this moment, your hands turn round so that your
palms, briefly facing downwards, turn outwards towards the
sky. In this movement of the hands you can feel a kind of bud
opening to the light. Your arms widen vertically above your
head and out into upper space. Your shoulder blades remain
expanded — it is as if wings grow from them and 'carry' the
movement of the arms. Your *bodyweight is now slightly inclined*

41

backwards, while the head is free and 'receives' the open space above it. A kind of heavenly dome is created directly above you, and this grows all the bigger the more you ensure that you retain and strengthen the inversion point at your centre as focus and anchor for space. In this way the heart becomes an organ of perception for your surroundings, with your arms as the heart's antennae.

Once your hands have reached the highest point, they move apart from each other sideways. The (soul) space continues to widen in the space between them even as the outward movement begins to wane again: the arms, spread out but relaxed, sink without tension to either side, and *your weight shifts back to the centre again.*

As your arms reach the horizontal level, gravity takes hold of them again; and then a new L can start — the hands themselves grasp hold of what grasps them . . .

Make sure that:

- the point of equilibrium swings: front — centre — back — centre — front, etc.;
- your knees are loose and can follow the flow of movement or give way to it;
- the movement remains flowing as the gesture arises and fades;
- there is inner equilibrium between centre and periphery.

Practice options:

- only moving your body, without gestures; or only inner movement (as the basis of every gesture);
- make the gesture very small, with your hands only in front of your heart (and yet still let the movement fill the whole space!);
- perform seven Ls in succession, making each one larger without losing inwardness as the gesture expands; then the

opposite – seven Ls that start large and keep growing smaller, making sure that inner breadth is retained in outwardly small movement;

- in several successive Ls, perceive the process and connection between them, and thus create an arc spanning the whole movement sequence;
- intensify the movement between back and front by standing with legs apart or by making several steps between front and back in the rhythm of the gesture;
- reverse the weight-swing, so that as you lead the gesture downwards you shift weight (or step) backwards. This gives breadth to the frontspace. As you lead the gesture upwards, you shift weight (or step) forwards, so that the backspace gains breadth. In this type of confluence of body movement and gesture you will need stronger activity since you are engaging here with a greater (counter)space.

Penetrating M

The sound M has the quality of connecting and absorbing. If we like a particular food, we say 'mmm', and in many languages this sound is contained in the word for mother, through whom we first discover the world. M expresses entering into something to experience it from within. At the same time it helps us to hold ourselves together if we are somewhat nervous or restless, have been working in too one-sided a way, or are seeking inner strength.

In the same way that our lips press down on each other feelingly to form M, so that the voice passes through them, in the M gesture the palms move towards each other in front of you, taking turns each time to pass from front and rear, the arms of course moving with them. The hands don't make contact in the middle, but pass each other by. Each perceiving hand pushes

Fig. 11 M

through and penetrates the air in its own stream, but with the other hand at the same time forms direction and counter-direction.

Try to feel in the wholeness of this gesture the density of the air, the substance of the world.

In order to penetrate something and experience its being and nature, we have to move towards and touch into it; for this reason the movement is not simply light and effortless but meets a sense of resistance — which comes to expression in the gesture as direction and counter-direction.

Once you have penetrated and 'tasted' what you are trying to perceive, the movement comes to rest, and is held for a moment in form. Then the hands change direction and once again pass each other by in a new sensing gesture. Repeat this several times.

The upper body moves naturally with this, scarcely visibly but in a more 'hearkening' way, led by feeling into the stream of the M.

Now you can also involve the legs. Stand with your feet one behind each other, or even slightly crossed so that the back knee leans into the groove of the front one if you gently bend your knees.

Now slightly bend your knees as just described as you do an M gesture with your arms. It is like a pushing together. When you can't go any further, retain the arm gesture but with your legs give an impulse from behind as follows. Relax the back leg very slightly from its purchase and push into the front one so that it

44

slightly springs forward. Your weight briefly shifts to your back leg. Then stand again on your front leg and draw the back one towards it—and then you are in the starting position again.

Practice options:

- Instead of bending your knees you can hop: stand on your front leg and push the knee of the back leg directly into the groove of the front one, but without first bending the knee. Both legs are more or less straight. The impetus sends the front leg forwards and your weight shifts to the back leg, which is now standing as the front leg swings forward. But now the front leg swings back so that its knee groove meets the knee of the back leg again—this gives rise to a back-and-forth swinging or hopping movement, in which the front leg remains in front and the back leg behind. The upper body remains relatively still throughout. In eurythmy this is called the 'peewit' step.

- Now you can add the arm gesture of the M to this—*one* arm gesture in which the hands pass each other once, to about four swinging motions with the legs, so that you strike the front leg twice with the back leg, and the back leg twice with the front leg.

B to counteract migraine and other headaches[*]

The B sound creates enclosure and protection. In Hebrew, Beth (ב) means 'house'. The B gives me the certainty that I am safe within myself because something greater gives me to myself. In this specific exercise one gathers forces that are rising too strongly upwards and reconnects them as if in a mantle with our lower organism, thus enabling the head to be free.

---

[*] The 'migraine B' is also a eurythmy therapy exercise. If one wishes to use it therapeutically it is advisable to find a eurythmy therapist.

Important: The migraine B should not be done *during* acute migraine or other severe headaches, but at times when you do not have a headache. Then it should be done intensively.

Fig. 12 B — *movement sequence*

Fig. 13 B — *gesture in kneeling*

Reach down with your arms and hands into the space behind you, with your palms facing forwards. Imagine you are taking hold of a blue cloak, which you bring forward and wrap yourself in — not tightly, but so that you create an inner space. As you do this your hands turn so that the palms are always facing your body. The arms together with the shoulder blades create the form of an enveloping gesture, within which your whole form is safe and protected: your shoulders, back, arms, stomach and internal organs. Within this mantle, however, an upright stance is maintained from legs to head, connected with the heart, a bright 'yellow' column. The imagined mantle of blue protects this light, for the B is not a dark sound — it has an inward, light-filled, free and mobile quality.

Now, while forming the B

gesture, with feet together, kneel down as far as you can (you can at the same time go slightly on tip-toes to spare pressure on the knees). Once you are in the knee-bend, and have at the same time formed the B gesture, release this and raise yourself lightly and not too fast, like a phoenix from the ashes.

Repeat this around ten times.

Make sure that:

- when you bend your knees and afterwards straighten your legs again, you move all the time within a column of light both as you descend and ascend again (this column passes through your spine);
- you do not curve your back but form a mantle only through the gesture of the arms;
- that you do not lift your feet from the ground when you rise again but keep strong contact with it through the soles of your feet.

Rhythmic R*

The R is a fricative which rolls on the air. It gives us air to breathe because it creates a movement that rhythmically connects inner and outer. The R enlivens, activates and has a refreshing quality.

Stand upright, and draw your vertically upward-pointing upper arms sideways towards you so that the palms are facing forwards beside your shoulders. Then bend your upper body forward and in a swinging motion engage your arms also in this developing 'involution'. Here the arms—*briefly* also straightening—fly in a wave that passes upwards, forwards, downwards and back, so that your hands come to rest below the upper arms. The head follows this movement, and also bends.

---

*The rhythmic R is also a eurythmy therapy exercise. If one wishes to use it therapeutically it is advisable to find a eurythmy therapist.

Then swing your upper body back; let your arms follow the movement again. They fly forward, straighten as they fly upward and, when the upper body is standing upright again (and almost over-straightened), are drawn back again into the starting position.

This creates a swinging of the upper body back and forth between straightening and bending, while at the same time the arms fly outwards with the upper body's movement and are drawn back in the 'pauses' between it. Take care that in this pendulum motion you create, at the same time, a breathing rhythm between impulse — movement — pause; (new) impulse — movement — pause. We can really experience this as a form of breathing: the R is breathed in and out. The soul accompanies this, like the arms giving itself up to the element of air, though the physical breath is not explicitly tied to the outward movement.

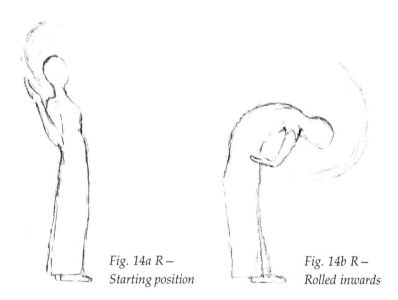

Fig. 14a R –
Starting position

Fig. 14b R –
Rolled inwards

6. The Heart — An Organ of Perception for Destiny

Heart, you soul-bearer,
Your light's spirit force
Conjures life from
Immeasurably deep within us.[12]

Rudolf Steiner

The heart knows no 'normal' or 'usual' condition, nor any sense of 'this is how we do things'. It knows neither principles nor standards. The heart seeks relationship; it is the place where every connection or relationship finds its purpose. It wishes to open to this. Relationship is destiny, whether from the past or for the future.

The heart is a gateway and also a key. But it is our being that can turn the key, open the door and step through. To strengthen heart forces means to encourage our own being to find trust in our own powers and engage warmly in life. To purify the heart means giving our own being the ability to enter into the world unhindered, whether this be the visible or invisible world. To widen the heart means to give our own being space so that it can increasingly identify with the whole world.

Exercise: Sun power in the human heart (contracting and releasing)

Stand or sit so that the weight of your body is inclined forward, and bending so that you can at the same time feel an inner space which this bending forms. The arms are drawn in close towards you, the

49

hands are laid over each other to create a small interior space in front of the heart. Within this space feel the light of the sun.

Now try to picture a sunrise inwardly and vividly. The upper body opens, the hands and arms open outwards with the rays of the heart's sun, until you are, in the full midday sun, as it were, looking upwards to the zenith, and completely given up to the light. Your form is now almost overstretched; the arms and hands extend upwards on either side, and the whole front of your body itself radiates light.

Now feel how the sun's motion turns; the blue of the heavens grows deeper, and the sun once more approaches you. Try to initiate this turning point in your feeling, and then you will immediately sense how tension is released in your form and you again receive the light until the sun vanishes as it were below the horizon, into you yourself, and night comes again. Now you are bending once again, and within you interior space is created, in which the light shines towards you as if from the other, spiritual side.

Here again there is a turning point, which you must sense in great tranquillity within your deepest inner being. The light begins to grow from there anew into the world, and you start once again to straighten and stretch...

This gathering and releasing can be done several times in succession. It can also be done in miniature, with only the upper body and hands, and it can intensify in outward movement; or you can let the light shine out several times in all grandeur and then fade again.

You can end this exercise by finding your way back from one of the turning points to the upright position. For a moment hearken to the echo or resonance of the exercise in you.

Contracting — releasing with a sphere

With one hand form a bowl in front of you, imagining that you are holding in it a sphere of warmth and light over which you protectively lay your other hand. This sphere of light and warmth is however *felt* within the heart, even if you encompass it outwardly with your hands. Now begin to breathe with this light-warmth sphere inwardly (not physically, or at least not intentionally). The light spreads out, the hands release themselves in the expanding warmth mantle around the sphere; 'encircle' it sideways and grasp it anew again so that the hand that was previously bearing the sphere now protects it and the one that was protecting it now bears it.

The sphere can return several times to its original size. But then, in several stages, you let it grow increasingly so that, as you 'encircle' it with the movements of your breath, you expand ever further into space with your arms. Ultimately you will be breathing so widely around your own form that your outspread arms 'touch' the horizon for a moment. The hands are sensors of the cosmic periphery within which

The lemniscate
The lemniscate is an ancient symbol and serves as the mathematical symbol for infinity. In following this form (∞) it becomes apparent that it creates an interior space in one half, which passing through the crossing point is inverted into outer space and vice versa. (This is easier to understand if you walk a lemniscate by following your nose and at the same time attend to one side of the body. The side of the body oriented to the mid-point of one half of the lemniscate becomes oriented to the space outside the form in the other half, after you pass through the crossing point.) The crossing point can be the symbol of many things, such as threshold, I being, gateway, death and becoming. It is the point where death becomes life and, in the other direction, where spirit transforms into matter.

It is also the point where an encounter occurs between two worlds. Else Klink, a eurythmist of the first generation, said that the lemniscate was an inwardly self-perceiving circle. The circle too is a picture of eternity, as
cont.

51

cont.
well as being an image of the self. In the lemniscate, eternity perceives itself—and that is the essence of the human being.

you stand for a moment like a cross before you lead this expanded breadth back to the heart centre again. The sphere now has a clear centre at the crossing point of the axes of space that pass through your own centre. In this way you will experience yourself standing upright and embedded within the whole cosmos as a free human being.

From here, in several breathing movements, you can find your way back to the outwardly small sphere in the human heart, within which, however, the whole cosmos has been 'breathed in'.

It is best if you follow the sphere and its expansion not with your gaze but your feeling, since otherwise it is difficult to pass from the outward view, still possible in the first stage of the exercise, to the inner one.

Exercise: scale in a lemniscate[*]

First do a *listening exercise*. If you play an instrument—or you can sing it too—let a scale resound in space.

Scale

Every scale is clearly divided into two halves: the first four tones and then the following four. It is very easy to feel this division:

---

[*] Besides speech eurythmy (visible speech) there is also tone eurythmy (visible song). In tone eurythmy, too, we encompass inner laws—in this case those of music. In the structure of the human body we can find many musical relationships whose dynamic eurythmy can release and make manifest (see endnote 13).

- Starting from the base note, play or sing the next tone in the sequence, and then return to the base note;
- then play or sing to the third and return again;
- then to the fourth and back;
- finally sing or play up to the fifth and – can you return again? How does this feel? And how does it feel if you give free rein to the inner impetus and now sing or play further up to the octave?

Between the fourth and the fifth we cross a threshold at which something comes towards us from the other direction, and towards which we feel drawn. As long as we do not cross this threshold and, if you like, as yet know nothing of the 'light' of the octave, we feel quite at home in the lower half of the scale, which mantles us in a certain warmth. But as soon as we cross the threshold into the light from the octave, we experience 'being at home' or 'coming home' at a new level, and strive towards it.

We can likewise experience this threshold very clearly in a descending scale. From the fourth onwards we again feel ourselves fully encompassed in the base note, which seems to await and expect us.

Lemniscate

As you begin the exercise, imagine you are standing midway between back- and frontspace in a lemniscate moving in the sagittal plane, whose crossing point lies in your heart (see following pictures). Then with your arms you follow the stream of the 8. From the feet it arches forwards and collects in the heart; there you can experience something like a pulse beat into a new space, one that now opens backwards. Within this, the stream arches up over the head, until you can experience the zenith directly above you. From there it approaches you again, arches forwards, inverts in the heart and then streams backwards down to the feet again. You now receive the stream.

Figs 15a–15f Lemniscate in the sagittal plane

During the exercise, the whole form moves backwards and forwards with this motion.

Lemniscate and scale

This lemniscate as just described now serves as the basis for the scale. The movement remains the same, except that you embed it in the stream of the scale. Inwardly sing the scale up to the zenith, and from there down again until you reach the base note. You stand as a human being between heaven and earth, and you yourself are the scale. The 'threshold' is your own heart. It is there that the lower tetrachord passes over into the upper, and vice versa. The heart keeps opening a space anew, perceiving what is coming and accompanying what develops.

In this way you can learn to rest at the two endpoints — base note and octave — and discover that the stream does not stop but neither does anything *impel* you onwards. In the base note, connect through your feet with the earth, and in the octave connect with your higher self in the light above your head. At both points you can receive the exercise anew, or also end it there, placing yourself finally midway between both energy points and feeling your upright stance and your open heart between these two poles.

Through the lemniscate, through the in- and out-streaming, through the heart as threshold between two very different spaces which in turn invert into each other through the heart, we place ourselves into the picture of the human being as a spiritual and physical being who draws his impulses — each night and in every life anew — from the world of spirit into his earthly existence; and then bears the fruits of this back again.[13] By placing yourself into this picture and experiencing its reality, its life forces become available to you.

Try to sense when the musical stream must make headway against resistance. When is it being 'pulled', and when received?

Exercise: Hallelujah

Hallelujah is the first word that was performed in eurythmy. It cleanses the soul and should also be eurythmically 'spoken' with this in mind. A purifying process is hidden in the word's very sounds. The L is the sustaining sound of the word; when it first comes it is intensified in seven stages, starting with a small gesture that expands continually and ends large. The second time the L comes, it is done three times in large, space-shaping gestures.

The vowels come before, between and after the L, and mark vivid stages on a path. The word begins and end with the H, a sound that can waft through spaces with spiritual power, making them fruitful and opening them.

The H is a sound that can be formed both by the out-streaming and in-streaming breath. In the word hallelujah the impulse in the initial H comes from within and streams outwards, whereas the final H is received from outside. Thus the H has two gestures. We begin with the first:

H:

Contract your arms and hands in front of the heart, creating a slight muscle tension between the hands and shoulder girdle; arms and upper body are rounded. You will know the release of energy when you say the sound H, and now you need this in the movement so as to cast off the whole tension that you have built

> **The human being – a scale between heaven and earth**
>
> By virtue of his 'bodies' and his I (four levels of reality in which he stands and which he incarnates) the human being himself is a scale between heaven and earth: he is connected with the earth in his physical body, with the plant world in his life body, and with the animals in his feeling body, extending up to the stars. In his I lives the divine spark.
>
> The physical and life body on the one hand, and the feeling body and the I on the other, have the same relationship with each other as the lower to the upper tetrachord of the scale.

57

up. With a single impulse open between your shoulder blades, relax your shoulders and upper arms, and let go of everything fixed, dark, burdensome: it flies away along the length of your arms which open freely and expansively upwards. Now you stand there upright.

A ('ah'):

Now tense your loose arms, straighten them and thus form an angle opening upwards. Your hands are open and straight, as the 'antennae' for light. Feel your whole self as a picture of this A ('ah').

Fig. 16 H –
Starting position

L:

Out of this A ('ah') now release the arms to form the L gesture and let this grow by stages as described above, 'brightening' ever further into space as you perform it seven times (for the L gesture see page 40).

E ('eh'):

Gather this process into a strong E ('eh') (see page 37). The E ('eh') can be done in front of the chest as a kind of boundary or, beginning below and gathering all the L's 'cloaks' together, can be formed above the head.

L:

Three large Ls now follow like a crown of light, a radiant surround within which you stand free and safe.

U ('oo'):

Gather this power of light once more in an U led from far below to far above by letting go of the final L, holding your arms

58

extended parallel downwards and raising them in front of you upwards to temple height, still straight and parallel. Take time for this but without inwardly interrupting the word.

J–A–H:

Now comes the concluding 'chord', J–A–H. Release one arm (release awareness from this arm and it will simply glide downwards) and, with the other, form a radiant I ('ee') upwards—you yourself are I ('ee') far above and beyond yourself! Then immediately pass on into an A ('ah') by raising and extending the other arm so that they form an angle together again—call up in yourself the sense of receiving the divine world in this vessel. Then free the tension of the A ('ah') first in your shoulders and then in your arms (as in the exercise A—reverence, p. 35) and in feeling only, without bending over, release this whole energy through yourself down towards the earth. Your arms relax and sink downwards to either side.

Finally form an E ('eh') by placing your crossed hands over your chest (palms pointing towards your body). This E ('eh') is also called the reverence E.

7. Consciousness Creates Reality

An action is always at the same time the locus where an intuition is received. One is not possible without the other, and only both together produce a work of art.[15]

Johannes Stüttgen

Any form of consciousness creates the reality corresponding to it. We do not stand separate from reality but are part of it. We not only experience it but *co-create and enliven it* at every moment through our consciousness. I interpret every situation in life and thus give it meaning. But the important thing is my interpretative direction: do I experience a situation as *useful for* or *a consequence of* something? Did I have a difficult childhood because of my problems with my mother, or was it so that I could experience something that helps me in my subsequent career? Has my life been ruined because I lost my job and have to leave a familiar place, or does this event give me the opportunity to reflect on what is really important to me? Do I look at life from the perspective of the past or the future? Do I just see what I have become or can I intuit what I wish to be? Some people go under in difficult situations while others discover their intrinsic strength through them.

Our inherent strength enables us to take hold of a situation and not merely succumb to the blows of fate.

In eurythmy, however, we do not interpret but *become active* out of our inmost core of being, learning to experience and strengthen the self as the source of thinking, action and existence. We can open up new paths to the reality we wish to create, and in doing so future potential can be experienced in the here and now — as what we ourselves can bring into the world by our own powers.

The following exercises aim to send consciousness ahead of physical movement, so that we ourselves open the spaces into which we wish to enter. To change from one position to the next, from one direction to another, we must engender will impulses and intentions. Interestingly, these already become visible to others when we grasp them spiritually. The question of inner and outer, spirit and matter, always arises anew and is immediately answered by engaged spiritual activity.

Exercise: I think speech

There is a drawing by Agrippa von Nettesheim (1486–1535), a German scholar, mystic and physician, which shows the human being in six positions assigned to star forces.

The following exercise is based on this. It is done in silence but you can inwardly speak the words that Rudolf Steiner gave

Fig. 17 Agrippa von Nettesheim: The Human Measure

many years later, or you can find other words and thoughts to accompany it. The positions themselves have a strong and eloquent effect.

It is assumed that these positions had long been practised before Agrippa drew them. Rudolf Steiner took them up again as a spiritual reality, but he reversed the sequence of the first two positions. Agrippa passes, as it were, from the stars to the cross: the cosmic light dies into the physical body. In Steiner's version we pass from the cross form into illumination *from within*, to the 'star position' whose line passes through the larynx. In this sequence, in the context of eurythmy, they are more fitting for modern people, and their meaning acquires a different emphasis.

Stand with feet together for the starting position. Standing upright, form the cross position inwardly in your mind. Then raise your arms sideways from the shoulder blades into the horizontal position: *I think speech.*

Then very slightly move your right foot sideways while your arms rise just a little upwards (all movement between the positions, except for the last, occur sideways) so that your hands are now at the level of the larynx. Do not perform the movement in a merely 'technical' way but experience it arising from the strength at your centre, which places itself with full awareness into the midst of life: *I speak.*

In the third position you open the leg position still further by moving the left foot further outwards. It is now like a great outbreathing: lower your arms until your hands arrive at the level of your heart: *I have spoken.*

This concludes the first triad, which forms an inward unity. It is connected more with the earthly realm and also with the frontspace.

The next triad is oriented more to spiritual space. A great inversion occurs between the third and fourth position. Here an entirely new resolve has to be made.

Once again move the *right* foot still further out, while the arms, whose movement again starts in the shoulder blades, move upwards until the same angle forms above as below. (In this position you can hold your hands turned downwards or upwards.) You thus form a cross of diagonals. The more deeply you connect downwards, the higher up you reach, and become free above: *I seek myself in the spirit.* (Here one ought really almost to feel: I seek myself in the spirit by *passing through* matter.)

Then bring the powers from the world of spirit back down into the earthly world (if necessary turning the hands downwards again) but remain connected with the spiritual periphery. The arms — kept straight — are lowered until the hands come to rest at the level of the temples. The left foot is drawn back towards the right, though the feet are still apart: *I feel myself within myself.*

To reach the final position, the only larger movement of the sequence now follows. Release the arms sideways and lower them to a downward parallel, close the feet (by drawing the right foot in) and then raise the arms parallel in front of you through all zones, and staying connected with them all, until you create the form of a pillar: *I am on the way to the spirit, to myself.*

Aspects to consider:

- Frontspace, backspace.
- Alternating between 'outbreath' and 'inbreath' of the gesture in raising and sinking of the arms.
- Where does the inner impulse take hold of the physical body? In the shoulder blades, in the heart, the feet?

Practice options:

- Leap from one position to the next (without words, only the positions). Do this in a slow tempo but also really fast, at least three times in succession.

- Pass from one position to the next in the tempo of your inner focus on the words or the gestural language of the positions.
- Stay for a long time in one position, performing each one like a meditation. You can increase from day to day (or week to week) the length of time you stay in a position, so that your muscle strength begins to correspond to the spiritual energy.

Exercise: We seek the soul—the spirit shines towards us

As the title of this exercise already tells us, there are two kinds of activity involved here, each of which is qualitatively different. We can use the image of point and periphery for this: the first part starts with the point and prepares to open itself up to the periphery; the second part lives in the periphery and works back towards the point. If I enter into these forces and try to encompass them, the gateway opens to cosmic powers living within us.

At the same time our soul space expands if I try to spiritually grasp the form as a whole (in the earthly realm it arises in chronological sequence, but spiritually it is a unity). And ultimately the exercise refreshes us by a continuous passage through our own centre at the moments of inversion.

This exercise consists of the following form. Starting in a right-hand direction, move a simple inward spiral forward towards a point that lies straight in front of you. From there you move backwards, again in a right-hand direction, in a simple inward spiral backwards, back to your starting point. The spiral can be drawn out a little length-wise (see drawing).

Fig. 18 Inward spiral forwards and backwards

Now it is interesting to simply walk this form a couple of times. Here you can attend to the following:

- Is the forward spiral different from the backward one?
- At what point is it clear that it will be a spiral?
- What happens at the starting points behind and in front? And does the same thing happen at both places?
- Where is the place—in space, in me, and if in me, where exactly?—where the form finds its new direction?

As you move the form you can inwardly (silently) speak the words, 'I seek the soul, the spirit shines towards me.' Or, 'We seek the soul, the spirit shines towards us.'

If you try to grasp this form as a thought—which is what we really do when we follow it in movement and perception—then you will conclude that there is a clear difference between the back and front spiral. In a forwards direction my perception is more inwardly directed, more strongly gathered and focused; space is rounded. In a backward direction, it is as if the whole back of my body, starting from the shoulder blades, flowed sideways into a broad surface—into a golden ground, as in medieval paintings. It is a free space that surrounds me and into which I enter as free being. My back, neck and the back of my head are 'open', and with my hands I can effortlessly reach upward into space.

In this way you can accompany both forms with a gesture. In front it is a movement that integrates space into itself, from the wide periphery towards the heart. Behind, the movement touches into the space of light behind and over you, in a certain sense not creating but bearing witness to it. (If you are already familiar with eurythmy, and you know the various speech-sound gestures, try to incorporate vowels into the forward spiral, and shape the space consonantally as you spiral backwards.)

But what happens, or what do you do, at the points where you form the impetus for a new direction?

Inwardly you open a gateway to these spaces described above. *You yourself are this gateway through which something new can form and also reveal itself: you yourself create the path into the world.* Precisely this is the activity needed in eurythmy. It is a creative art because your being must become creative to render reality, relationships, correspondences visible, shaping and perceiving them.

Exercise: Five-pointed star

The human form

The Five-pointed star is inscribed in the human form. As in the third position of the exercise, 'I think speech', you can place your human figure into the Five-pointed star. And then you can sense a stream that connects the star's five points with each other:

From the head to the right foot,
from the right foot to the left hand,
from the left hand to the right hand at heart level,
from the right hand to the left foot
and from the left foot back to the head.

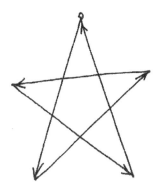

Fig. 19 See Fig. 17

Fig. 20 The five-pointed star in the human form

Forms in space

Before you move the form in space, inwardly picture the five-pointed star in a way vivid enough to follow.

If you now project this star into space, start at the head point. If I drew the form on the ground this point would be behind. Thus you should inwardly move the form *forwards* to the 'feet', or more precisely to the right-hand foot point, from the point furthest behind. From there lead it further in your mind at an angle backwards to the left-hand point, then horizontally right to the right-hand point, then at a left angle *forwards* to the left foot, and again *backwards* to the head point.

Now actually move the form: take three to five steps for each direction. Once you have the five-pointed star inwardly as a picture and outwardly as a form, you can reduce the number of steps, and form the star with only one step per direction. Make sure that your head is always directly above you feet so that your whole form goes with the swift changes of direction, and that a form really is created in space (rather than simply walking lines on the floor).

The raying form can give you a sense of creating a light ray passing from infinity to infinity, the straight lines being far, far longer than is visible in the physical realm. And each new infinity, or eternity, comes towards us at the moment we encompass it in our minds.

Five-pointed star with light rays

If you now add the arm gestures, you can embody the form in space with light rays. The first direction

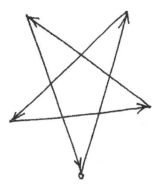

Fig. 21 The five-pointed star as path

leads from above downwards with the right arm like a ray of light from heaven to earth; then let this go below, and from bottom right receive a new ray with the left arm. Take this and lead it outwards in a left direction towards the horizon at heart level, where you again let go of it. Now receive a new ray from there with the right arm and after a horizontal journey to the right let go of it again. From the right, with your left hand, receive another ray that leads downwards to the left foot, until your left arm is extended and points to the earth. Finally, with your right arm receive a ray from bottom left and lead it back upwards to the head point which is situated above your head, in the light.

The hand or arm that releases one ray can keep that direction until it is needed again to conduct a new ray. Thus breadth arises between the two arms, and within this light can unfold.

Five-pointed star with I ('ee')

In a somewhat similar way you can use the sound I ('ee'). Unlike the 'light ray' exercise above, the I repeatedly arises anew from the heart as inner power. (A light ray, as described above, is something eternal and objective that belongs intrinsically to the form; an I ('ee') is a power from within, speaking out of the human being — individually — as eternity.)

On every path of the five-pointed star, form the I gesture anew, either letting it shine out as archetypal gesture *between above and below* or, using only one arm, forming it in each different direction of the star: downwards, horizontally or upwards.

8. Fully Present in Life

Good only comes when we create it.

Erich Kästner[16]

The title of this chapter corresponds very well to the first exercise, in which you do indeed place yourself fully into the midst of life. Try to retain the presence of mind you thereby acquire in the other exercises too. These are concerned with independence and are built up in such a way that, gradually, one after another movement is added. It is hard to conceive of performing their whole multiplicity, but in the immediacy of practice they can be done. Most people will need to work hard until they master them, yet the greater context that gradually emerges through them consists in the growth of inner space and freedom.

Then we are fully present in our lives. If our soul is really present in physical experience, we can experience abundance and beauty. If we encompass existence with our spirit, we can act effectively. But just as inner or mental exercises do not impose interpretations but only strengthen you to find your own direction, so these exercises do not give abundance either, by themselves, but rather the capacity to acquire riches. Eurythmy creates the instrument. You yourself can and must play it.

Exercise: Descending seventh

The interval of the seventh from the base note is a transition between the interval of the sixth and the octave, or from the octave to the sixth. This interval is very close to the octave's completion and culmination, and full of the expectation of reaching this. This tension and expectancy is life force, a kind of inner suction. In the reverse direction, away from the octave, the seventh has to pull itself away from this suction, but takes with it the fullness of the octave. If we leap directly from the seventh to the base note, we can absorb this substance without the loss that our passage through the other intervals would otherwise cause.

Stand upright, feet together, and let your arms hang loose. Now stretch your arms forwards and upwards, so that your hands are in front of you and a little above head height. Now leave the hands where they are while you pull yourself forward towards them by taking a step; in doing so you will bend your arms (the hands keep pointing forward) without lowering them. Having taken one step forward, pull your back foot forward too so that your feet are together once again. Only now do you let your arms sink down beside your body. That is the technique of the exercise.

Fig. 22 Descending seventh

But now sense *within* these physical movements that you are extending your arms into a fullness and wealth of life that you have previously created, and that under your arms a kind of cushion of air develops. When you bend your arms, perceive this life force which you draw into you through the air cushion, as you move a step towards it, in upright stance, to absorb it. It streams down through your form.

You can perform this movement slowly, and thus awaken the substance, sensing and touching into it. And you can do this several times in succession.

Exercise: Dexterity E ('eh')

Cross your outstretched arms so that the lower arms make strong contact; alternate between having the right and left arms uppermost.

Cross your arms four times: once over your head, then horizontally in front of you, then diagonally downwards in front of you, and finally behind you.

Now, at the same time, to accompany each contact of the two arms, place a heel at the place directly below the knee of the other leg. Do this in alternation too: right heel, left heel, or left knee, right knee.

You can repeat this at least three times and quicken the tempo as you do so; and then perform the movements slowly again.

As the name of the exercise tells us, this exercise gives dexterity and mobility. If you remain inwardly calm, but present as you do it (despite increasing the movement's intensity) this has an enlivening effect on the soul, on the one hand, and also creates inner certainty and strength.

Step exercises

Step exercises aim to bring awareness into the feet. Short steps and long ones together create a rhythm: .. means short short; — means long.

A short step is about half a foot long, while a long step is a good foot in length. The tempo relationship corresponds to the length: the short step lasts only half as long as the long step, and

Fig. 23 Dexterity E ('eh')

71

can be done by touching the ground only with the front of the foot.

1)

$$. . - - - / - . . - - / - - . . - / - - - - . .$$

(thus: short, short, long, long, long/etc.), then the same backwards:

$$- - - . . / - - . . - / - . . - - / . . - - - -$$

You can also replace two short steps with one stamp or hop; the stamp or hop then has the length of a long step, so that a 4/4 tempo is again created.

2)

Take the following steps, *each within the same time unit*:

one step forward
two steps backward
three steps forward
four steps backward
five steps forward
six steps backward
seven steps forward

and then:

six steps backward
five steps forward
four steps backward
three steps forward
two steps backward
one step forward

In the first part, as the number of steps increases, they grow ever shorter, and in the second part, as the number of steps reduces, they lengthen. This exercise also concerns an inner unity of measure that encompasses the number of (either forward or backward) steps on a path. If you achieve this 'unity in action' you will increasingly experience yourself as a unity, for inner and outer are one.

In this exercise also try to attend to the counterstream: as you step forward be aware of the space becoming more expansive behind you; and when you step backwards, experience the breadth thus created in front of you.

Independence exercises

These are exercises in which the feet obey a rhythm different to that of the hands, for instance when clapping.

1)

Start with an exercise consisting of simple counter-rhythms: move $-$ . . (long short short) while clapping . . $-$ (short short long).

2)

A more difficult variant of this could be as follows:
With your feet move the following rhythm:

. . $-$ $-$ $-$ / $-$ . . $-$ $-$ / $-$ $-$ . . $-$ / $-$ $-$ $-$ . .

Once you can do this easily, practise the following clapping rhythm

$-$ $-$ $-$ . . / $-$ $-$ . . $-$ / $-$ . . $-$ $-$ / . . $-$ $-$ $-$

Freedom or independence involves being able to do both these at once.

3)

You can also do exercise 2 from the previous step exercises, taking from one to seven steps in the same unit of time. But now also accompany this with *one* arm gesture, irrespective of whether you are taking one or seven steps.

Between your hands held vertically, form a sphere (similar to the starting position for the exercise 'contracting – releasing with a sphere', page 50). But here you form the sphere by enclosing it back and front instead of from above and below. The hands do not touch. Open the sphere upwards, keeping the wrists close together, then turn the hands past each other and close the sphere again.

It does not matter whether you form the sphere above your head, in front of your chest or below, but each variant has a different quality.

Make sure that:

- you remain upright, and that the more steps you take, the more mobile and dynamic the path becomes;
- you remain inwardly tranquil.

4)

Do the variant with arm movements in the three planes of space referred to in the chapter 'Every Person Wears a Crown' (p. 20). There you will find the following practice options:

- In standing perform the arm movement in 'canon', i.e. begin for instance by raising the right arm from below into the horizontal plane, and start with the left arm when the right arm embarks on the second direction.
- Do the same in walking.

This is also an 'independence' exercise.

9. Wholeness Within Polarity

The following exercises require an inner power of vision and certainty in so far as the form as a whole is concerned, an inner 'overview'. This is something quite different from having an 'angle' or 'perspective', which is more to do with looking at something externally, from a one-sided point of view. We become inwardly seeing when, through our own activity, we ourselves begin to create a whole picture. It is this inner activity that is able to raise my body into the lightness of movement.

The idea is the starting point—and as long as you look at the diagrams on pages 78 and 81 in an external way only, you won't get beyond this. The idea still stands *before* me. This is also why ideas often collide with reality, since they have not yet been fully imbued with feeling and life. Is what I picture right? Can it be lived? Now—both in life itself and in the following exercises—we need perception. In relation to eurythmy this means that I first feel the idea through my form, I absorb it into me and, perceiving it, begin to move. With my feeling I sense its nature, and move 'along' the thought (which is revealed in form). As I do so this gradually gives rise to an inner picture, a totality. And now I am ready to move the form in space.

In the following forms, their wholeness also arises through the alternation between straight and rounded movement sequences. In this alternation we can sense that we must continually take new hold of ourselves.

A straight line has its direction implicit in its beginning. It helps me to clarity through the quality intrinsic to it because, within it, passing through my centre, I orientate myself between two poles. Once I have decided on a direction, it continues as it

75

is, and I continue within it.
The straight line has an aim
and target, and remains
'faithful to its beginnings',
determined by an arrange-
ment of points that connect it,
but beyond which it extends
further.

Curved forms, on the other
hand, form an inner or outer
space and are at the same time
in creative motion. A round or
curved form renews itself in
every point! Here the will is
uninterruptedly at work in
embarking on a new direction,
developing and shaping it.

Where straight and curved
forms alternate, this intensi-
fies my capacity to adapt my
inner outlook, since my whole
human existence requires
movement. Having adopted a
particular 'principle', immediately we have to revise our
view again . . . This represents
a particular strengthening of
the life forces.

Exercise: Cross form with circle

Stretch both your arms vertically upwards, turning your palms
forward. Feel yourself standing in the frontal plane, which

divides front from back. Now lower your extended arms slowly to your sides in this plane and feel the circle that your hands describe and within which you stand.

Now begin again from above and form the circle actively with the left hand which, starting at the left, describes a semicircle sideways and downwards. The right hand performs the same movement after an interval, following the motion of the left hand on its own side but without awareness focused on it. Only when it arrives at the very bottom does it take over the circling current from the left hand, now raising it sideways again to the zenith. The left arm follows, and is also led sideways and upwards without directing any particular attention to it. But always try to sense the wholeness of the movements.

Now create a cross within the circle. From above bring both hands to the heart, and from there lead them horizontally left and right into the periphery. Bring them back in again and lead them straight down in front of you. From there lead them back to the heart once more and then again horizontally sideways into the periphery; and finally, bring them back to the heart centre and upwards again. Independently of the physical movement, you can once again focus your awareness more on left or right.

In this movement you can now let straight and curved forms follow each other in alternation. For instance, start at top left and make a semi-circle downwards (round form). Then lead your right hand (with your left, if you like, following and accompanying this movement) from below up to the heart, and

In eurythmy we try to develop an inner space and to fill rather than assert its boundaries. This space is inviolable from without: no one else can take possession of it or make use of it, for we ourselves are this space. Eurythmy does not illustrate or embody either the point or the periphery but through it these become, rather, modes of existence in which we learn to dwell, and which thus become accessible to us from within.

77

from there out towards the right periphery (straight form, albeit in two parts). From the right a curved path again begins towards the left, passing through the zenith. From the zenith the left arm takes over the movement and completes it. Now take a straight path again to the heart and from there downwards (this time your awareness is focused on your left hand, and the right merely follows and accompanies it). And this is succeeded by a curved path: from below upwards via the right, make a semi-circle with your right arm. Above, the left arm again takes over, making a straight path to the heart, and then out into the left periphery (with the right arm accompanying). Then a curved path to the right, passing below, is begun by the left arm and ended by the right ... The last path is straight: it leads (with both arms, though the focus is on the right) from the right periphery to the centre and then back up to the zenith.

Throughout the exercise maintain your centre as calm pole, and feel the breadth that encircles this centre...

Having practised this, project into space the form you have accomplished with your arms in standing: what is uppermost in the gestures will be in the backspace, and what is below will be in the frontspace.

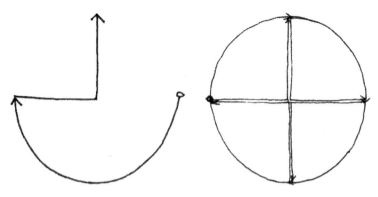

Figs 24a, 24b Cross and circle

First just practise walking a circle; the following points of external technique are important. Make sure:

- that your feet always point forwards, rather than following the *line* of the circle;
- that your shoulders are loose but always remain frontal, that is, parallel to the front of the circle space.

If you observe these two points rigorously, and follow your inner image of the circle (rather than its line), subordinating your sequence of steps (combination of open and crossing steps, moving forwards or backwards and to right or left) to the frontality principle, you will, with a little practice, succeed in creating a good circle.

Then place the cross form into this circle, once again beginning behind (corresponding to the upper gesture): behind — centre — left — centre — in front — centre — etc.

The paths of the cross are calmer, those of the circle more dynamic.

Then, in the same way as for the gestures, you can alternate between the forms of cross and circle. As soon as possible, do both the gesture and form at the same time.

Make sure that:

- the centre of the cross is always your own centre, both in inner and outer terms;
- the straight line is not simply a line, but that light manifests in it;
- each form lends space a distinctive quality.

Practice options:

- Having practised the forms with steps — e.g. three steps for each of the straight lines, eight smaller steps for the semicircle curve — you can gradually diminish the external movement and move through forms with an ever more inward dynamic; the middle of the cross remains your own centre.

- Practise the straight lines with counterstream, i.e. when you move outwards along them, maintain the inner centre irrespective of whether it lies behind you, beside you or in front of you. Likewise, when you move back along a straight line towards the centre, let the breadth of the periphery become visible by 'harnessing' your awareness between periphery and centre. When you are at the centre you have the greatest periphery. Or, in other words, someone at one with themselves is open to others and otherness. Here by way of illustration, is a poem by Christian Morgenstern:

> Everything in the end finds its fulfilment,
> as long as you can patiently await it,
> and give your growing joy the plentiful
> time it needs to reach maturity.
>
> Until one day at last you sense
> the rich scent of the ripened grain
> and opening yourself can bear the harvest
> into its deep granaries.[17]

Exercise: Five-pointed star with circle

Incorporate into the two following forms the structure of the five-pointed star as basis (see page 66). The 'sequence' of straight lines is interrupted by the curved forms: you begin with one straight line but this is followed by a curved one. At the point to which the curved form leads you, begin again with another straight line of the five-pointed star.

Thus you begin with a straight line from the head to the right foot of the star, then follow a curved path along the *pentagon* to the next star point; the second straight path will take you back from the left foot to the head. If you apply the principle of alternating between straight and curved lines consistently, at the

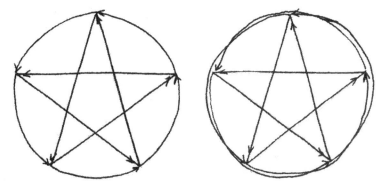

Figs 25a, 25b Five-pointed star with circle

end you will arrive back on a curved path at the head of the star. The same applies to the second form variant.

In both variants you can also do a vowel on the straight lines and a consonant such as L on the curved forms. By doing so you bring your whole body into the form. Remain upright—you should feel yourself in creative command of this.

10. Resilience in Daily Life: Spirit-imbued Matter

Soon no inch of our interior space will remain untrampled each and every day. Love, yes, even love ... becomes an external performance... None of this would be too bad if people were only machines. But it turns out they are something else, since they possess an I. And this I has its own laws. In other words: the I has certain conditions for growth. It is nourished solely by the motions it makes itself.[18]

Jacques Lusseyran

The word 'exercise' so often used in this booklet may give the impression that eurythmy ultimately leads to skill in what has been practised. That is certainly also the case. But more important than this is the engagement and inner activity, the engendering of pictures even if I already 'know' them in advance. Repeatedly it is a matter of bringing idea and perception into harmony with feeling, action and execution. This is something that has to be actively done, otherwise it fails to happen. The unity thus achieved only exists by virtue of activity. Then it can give you strength throughout the day and peace for the night; it can encourage, enliven and strengthen you in your engagement with the world. You see, we ourselves create the world.

Spirit-imbued matter is what we are if we find ourselves as spirit in the core of our being — in matter and through it, enlivening it. (And not the other way round, as if the spirit were a mere reflection of physical processes, as science assumes with its gaze entirely taken up by the level of reality that we call the physical.)

In the following compilation of exercises, you will find suggestions—not set programmes—that 'function'. If you find an exercise that seems fitting for your situation, or constitution, or state of health, then do it—feel free to search and try things out.

Exercise units

For the morning

I A O in standing (p. 14)
I think speech; positions with words, then leaping from one position to the next (p. 61)
Yes—No (p. 33)
Independence exercises (p. 73)

For the evening

I think speech; positions with words (p. 61)
Hallelujah (p. 57)
Spiralling inwards and outwards (p. 31)
Scale in a lemniscate (p. 52)

For courage

I A O (p. 14)
Yes—No (p. 33)
Hope—U (p. 36)
Love—E (p. 37)
Threefold walking (p. 20)
Light streams upwards—weight bears downwards (p. 32)

For enlivening

I think speech; leaping between positions (p. 61)
Rhythmic R (p. 47)

Descending seventh (p. 69)
Dexterity E (p. 71)

For strengthening the self

Yes – No (p. 33)
Love – E (p. 37)
Five-pointed star with I (p. 68)
Alternation exercises (I think speech, p. 61; We seek the soul
... p. 64; five-pointed star p. 66)
Independence exercises (p. 73)

For strengthening the life forces

Cross form with circle (alternation between straight lines
and curves) (p. 76)
Descending seventh (p. 69)
Yes – No (p. 33)
A – reverence (p. 35)

For exhaustion

Finding the upright (p. 11)
Threefold walking (p. 20)
Cross form with circle very calmly and meditatively (p. 76)
A – Reverence (p. 35)
Hope – U (p. 36)
Spiralling inwards and outwards (p. 31)
Light streams upwards – weight bears downwards (p. 32)

For harmonization

I A O (p. 14)
Peewit M (p. 45)

Contracting – expanding with a sphere (p. 50)
Hallelujah (p. 57)

For calming

Flow in the step with arm movement in the three planes of space (p. 22)
Forms with counterstream (p. 31)
I think speech; positions with words (p. 61)
Contracting – expanding with a sphere (p. 50)

For relaxation

Rhythmic R (p. 47)
B to release tensions in the head and shoulders (p. 45)
Contracting and expanding (p. 49)
Scale in a lemniscate (p. 52)

To counteract screen/computer work

Rhythmic R (p. 47)
Arm movements in the three planes of space (p. 22)
Dexterity E (p. 71)
Peewit M (p. 45)
B to release tensions in the head and shoulders (p. 45)
I think speech; leaping from position to position (p. 61)

Appendix

Areas where eurythmy is used

Education

Eurythmy nourishes the human soul with pictures, teaching us to move from thinking through feeling to the will, strengthening our inner being and thus preparing us for an effective life instead of just 'real life', as it it called. It is therefore an important element of Waldorf pedagogy from infancy through to school-leaving age. If we are more deeply rooted in reality we are closer to ourselves, and this gives us courage for the future, inner freedom and security.

This is complemented by the social aspect which can also be of decisive importance. In education and also in the workplace, eurythmy is done together in collaborative groups in which mutual awareness and coordination are nurtured.

The workplace

Through eurythmy we can counteract increasing external pressures, compensating for narrow or linear work processes. Perception is schooled, awareness of the spaces *between* colleagues (team building) can develop, deadening thought processes can be enlivened to create new scope for ideas, the soul that is bound to the computer screen for hours at a time can be refreshed, and burn-out avoided. Eurythmy helps us to create inner space and to fill this with our own activity. It fosters collaboration and positive relationship. From the production line to company management level, eurythmy can make a unique contribution. Organizations will only be able to develop well if the people working in them can unfold their potential and stay healthy.

Medicine and therapy

As mentioned in Chapter 5, eurythmy is a healing art. The powers in speech sounds, as macrocosmic principle, act upon the human microcosm if we ourselves connect with them through our own will activity. This stimulates our physical body to become healthy, tuning it to the spiritual principle underlying us as archetype.

Stage work

Eurythmy is also a stage art—firstly because every process is an art and requires an artist to shape it, and secondly also through the power active in language and music. On the stage, eurythmy becomes visible speech and music. Yet ideally it is never *representation* but always *enactment*, a real occurrence in the moment. It is never intended as symbolic or metaphorical but always embodies essence and reality.

Further (possible) fields

For addiction problems

Someone who succumbs to dependency loses his I to the substance or activity (drugs, work, sport, etc.). Every addiction is bound up with a search for, or also avoidance of, deeper answers. Eurythmy can help us to become inwardly mobile again, and to regain the power to shape and determine our own life through our core being. In this sense eurythmy is also prophylaxis against addiction.

'Thinking in movement' in academic institutions

Thinking in movement has two aspects. On the one hand it means developing mobile thinking, but also that my thinking takes place where the movement itself unfolds — that is, not in my head but in the phenomenon itself, whether this be a physical, sensory one or a spiritually tangible one. English has expressions that encompass this, such as 'grasping' an idea (the hands) or 'pursuing' and 'following' a train of thought (feet). Since we think on our feet in eurythmy, it is an excellent activity for those who seek to solve the problems of our time.[19]

Music college

In this volume we only touched very briefly on tone eurythmy, but it enables us to encompass the element of music as a holistic experience informing the whole human being. The focus here is on questions such as: What movement lies between tones? How does a whole musical work arise? What makes a musical phrase or development audible? When I play a piece, can I incorporate into its beginning my awareness of how it ends? This will subtly alter its quality.

Notes

1. Rudolf Steiner, *Menschenfragen und Weltenantworten* (GA 213), Rudolf Steiner Verlag, Dornach 1987, p. 24; and *Über die astrale Welt und das Devachan* (GA 88), Rudolf Steiner Verlag, Dornach 1999, p. 41.

2. Rudolf Steiner, lecture of 4 June 1924 in: *Esoterische Betrachtungen karmischer Zusammenhänge*, Volume Two (GA 236), Rudolf Steiner Verlag, Dornach 1988, pp. 242ff.

3. Jacques Lusseyran, *Ein neues Sehen der Welt. Gegen die Verschmutzung des Ich*, Verlag Freies Geistesleben, Stuttgart 1993, pp. 65ff.

4. Ibid. p. 36.

5. The first and, in particular, the second conversation with Johannes Stüttgen in Flensburger Heft 1/2007 is very illuminating in relation to this exercise. Stüttgen speaks there of various aspects of the idea of freedom and the nature of the human being.

6. Rudolf Steiner, lecture of 24 June 1924 in: *Eurythmie als sichtbare Sprache* (GA 279), Rudolf Steiner Verlag, Dornach 1990, p. 49.

7. 'Friedenstanz' ('Welt und Mensch') in: Rudolf Steiner, *Wahrspruchworte* (GA 40), Rudolf Steiner Verlag, Dornach 2005, p. 161.

8. Rudolf Steiner, lecture of 8 April 1922, and answers to questions in: *Damit der Mensch ganz Mensch werde. Die Bedeutung der Anthroposophie im Geistesleben der Gegenwart* (GA 82). Rudolf Steiner Verlag, Dornach 1994, pp. 48ff and 228ff.

9. Time is my own organism. This can be experienced in the fact that time gives me a larger sense of myself than does space. In time, earlier and later are connected. Standing outside this stream, I can only perceive time in relation to space. But if I move within time, I can experience its pattern and structure, and therefore also myself, in a new manner.

10. In Dorian Schmidt's research into formative forces he discovered some very interesting things relating to eurythmy exercises (see Dorian Schmidt, *Life Forces – Formative Forces: Methodology for Investigating the Living Realm*, Hawthorn Press, 2013). He found that

spaces full of light and confidence open in 'Yes' whereas a dark wall interposes itself in 'No'. In the alternation between yes and no the experience resembled clear mountain air and freedom imbued with a sense of self-reliant responsibility.

11. Rainer Maria Rilke, 'Palm', in: *Aus Taschen-Büchern und Merk-Blättern: in zufälliger Folge*, Vol. 3 of *Aus Rainer Maria Rilkes Nachlass*, Insel, Wiesbaden 1950, p. 29.

12. From the verse 'Sun, you ray-bearer', November 1924, in: Rudolf Steiner, *Mantrische Sprüche. Seelenübungen II, 1903–1925* (GA 268), Rudolf Steiner Verlag, Dornach 1999, p. 109.

13. Armin J. Husemann, *Der musikalische Bau des Menschen*, Verlag Freies Geistesleben, Stuttgart 2003; Armin J. Husemann, *Der hörender Mensch und die Wirklichkeit der Musik*, Verlag Freies Geistesleben, Stuttgart 2010.

14. In Hebrew the word hallelujah means 'praise God'. J–A–H stands for God, whose name is not meant to be uttered in Judaism. The H is inaudible, but the spirit is present within it.

15. Johannes Stüttgen, 'Die Freiheitsstatue und die "Soziale Plastik" ', *Flensburger Heft* 1/2007, p. 28.

16. Beginning of the poem, 'Morals', in: *Doktor Erich Kästners Lyrische Hausapotheke: ein Taschenbuch*, Atrium Verlag, Basel 1936, p. 31.

17. Christian Morgenstern, 'Stilles Reifen', in: *Gedichte in einem Band*, Insel Verlag, Frankfurt am Main and Leipzig 2003, p. 621.

18. Jacques Lusseyran, *Ein neues Sehen der Welt. Gegen die Verschmutzung des Ich*. Verlag Freies Geistesleben, Stuttgart 1993, pp. 70ff.

19. Although it is focused completely on thinking itself, the book by Natalie Knapp, *Der Quantensprung des Denkens. Was wir von der modernen Physik lernen können*, (Rowohlt Taschenbuch Verlag, Hamburg, 2012) points clearly in this direction.